Walk With Me

the poetry of

Sharon Canfield Dorsey

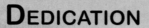

DEDICATION

I dedicate this book to my friend and publisher extraordinaire, Jeanne Johansen. Her expertise and insight have brought to life nine books for me, including four unique children's books. I will be forever grateful for her guidance and her sense of humor. After all, how many publishers would think bookworms, talking teacups, and a hermit crab could all be heroes?
Thank you, my friend.

WALK WITH ME

Walk with me through forests of morning
as dawn scatters a path of silver before us
and the future is young and limitless.

Walk with me through forests of midday
where heat blazes, tempering us, testing us
as we balance on the tightrope of middle age.

Walk with me through forests of evening
where sunset is still to come,
and wisdom is something to be shared.

Published by High Tide Publications, Inc.
www.hightidepublications.com

Thank you for purchasing an authorized edition of *Walk With Me*.

Edited by Cindy L. Freeman

Book Design by Firebellied Frog www.firebelliedfrog.com

Book Cover and inserts: Vivien Mann

Chapter Artwork: Kaye Levy

CHAPTER ONE

HOMAGE TO THE ANCESTORS

We are born…we live…we pass on.
Where did we come from?
Who came before us?
Knowing our heritage gives meaning to our lives.

ANCESTORS

2

We call them the ancient ones, the gatherers.
They vanished seven-hundred years ago,
leaving their stories in the mountain.

We follow steep trails, dug into rock by their hands,
to marvel at the grandeur of their cliff-top houses.

We discover pieces of their lives
in pottery shards and scraps of woven baskets.

We sense their souls in fading drawings
of people and animals on crumbling walls.

We envision tales of cunning and valor,
told 'round the stones of the blackened firepit.

A smudged handprint on a cave wall
reaches out to connect, beyond time and place.
They are our ancestors, spirits of the mountain.

Listen …
to the wind in the canyon,
and you will hear
echoes of songs,
whispers of stories,
silence in the waiting space
that is empty of life,
yet brimming with ghosts
of thousand-year struggles
in a deserted landscape -
weatherscape of sun and storm,
eternity of dawns and sunsets,
timescape of life past.

TIMELESS

3

BEING

INDIAN

4

Being Indian is not just a percentage of bloodline.
It is a feeling in your heart, connecting
you to Mother Earth, to the ancestors.

It's sitting beneath an ancient oak,
listening to the wind whisper to the leaves,
thanking the Great Spirit for his blessings.

It's marveling at the grandeur of a canyon,
the quiet whir of tiny hummingbird wings,
lightning dancing across a darkening summer sky.

It's shedding tears for concrete landscapes,
polluted air, and plastic-filled oceans.
Maybe that's not just being Indian.

Maybe that's being human.

Praise to the sun for its light and warmth;
Praise to the soil for cradling our crops;
Praise to the rains that nourish our fields;
Praise to the beasts whose sacrifice sustains us.

We thank you with our drums and voices.
We celebrate you with our dances.
We glorify you with our feathers and beads.
We acknowledge you with uplifted eyes.

We are one with the land, seas, and beasts.
We protect Mother Earth, our sacred cocoon,
aware that what affects one, affects all in the
                                    connected
                                                intertwined
                                                        cosmic chain.

CONNECTIONS

5

MY GREAT-GREAT-GRANDMOTHER

I wish I knew her story,
my great-great-grandmother, Martha.
She was Indian - full-blooded Cherokee,
who migrated to the Appalachian Mountains.

She married William, my great-great-grandfather,
a farmer, son of an Irish immigrant.
Together, they worked the land,
raised five children.

I study her photograph,
the high cheekbones,
the dark, straight hair,
the inscrutable staring eyes.

As a child, I was told I looked like her,
but nobody told me her story.
How and when did her family find their way
from North Carolina to West Virginia?

Did they escape from the infamous Trail of Tears?
Between four and eight thousand Cherokee died on that march.
She would have been ten years old at the beginning of the relocation
of sixteen thousand Indians from North Carolina to Oklahoma.

How terrified a ten-year-old would have been,
ripped from her home,
stripped of her possessions,
watching as it all went up in flames.

I located her name on the Cherokee identity rolls.
I have a faded copy of her tintype photograph.
I know she was born in 1828.

I wish, oh, how I wish, I knew the rest of her story.

Fancy Dancers twirl around the grassy arena,
feathers flying, a swirl of scarlet, turquoise and yellow.

Women in buckskin and beaded moccasins circle,
shawl-covered arms outstretched,
butterflies in slow motion.

Jingle Dress Dancers add treble to the bass of the drums,
their skirts, the instrument,
their undulating bodies, the artist.

Prairie Grass Dancers stealthily track unseen beasts,
brandishing bows and arrows
in an age-old fight for survival.

Painted faces reach upward
to the sunlight of the Great Spirit.
Native hearts reach backward, connecting to ancestors.

And beneath it all, the compelling pulse of the drums
pounds out the timeless heartbeat of my people.

Powwow

(HOMECOMING)

7

BEAR'S EARS...IT'S NOT JUST LAND

8

Bear's Ears National Monument in Utah is ancestral homeland
to the Hopi, Ute, Zuni Pueblo and the Navajo Nation,
beginning 13,000 years ago with the Clovis people,
predecessors of most indigenous cultures in the Americas.

100,000 archaeological sites of the Pueblo nations are embedded
in the steep cliffs, canyons and mesas of the 1.3 million-acre Monument.
Ancestors' bones lie there, dust to dust,
amidst the scraps of baskets, pottery and tools they left behind.

Our government proposes opening 88% of this sacred land
to pipelines, lumbering, and cattle grazing,
once again ignoring the treaties, contracts,
and promises made to native people.

Bear's Ears is not just land.
It is a centuries-old sacred burial ground.
Arlington Cemetery is also a sacred burial ground.
Would our government dig a pipeline through Arlington?

They gather on the National Mall
in Washington, DC,
twenty-five thousand strong,
indigenous people from throughout
the Western Hemisphere,
representing four hundred twenty tribes,
in full buckskin, beads, and feather regalia,
to honor and celebrate
the opening of the National Museum
of the American Indian.

A wrinkled Cherokee grandmother tells me,
"The spirits of the ancestors march with us today,
the spirits of the sixty-three million native people,
murdered to make way for civilization."
I believe her, feel their presence,
mourn their pain with my tears.

The Native Nations procession stretches
from the Washington Monument to the museum.
The alphabetical list of tribes fills six pages.
Aztec...Chickahominy...Hopi...Sioux... Zuni...
twenty-five thousand stand in place
under a blazing sun for hours,
drumming, chanting--families with children,
ancient ones in wheelchairs.

The end of the procession takes three hours
to arrive at the museum.
No matter the wait or the walk.
The journey to this moment has taken centuries.
At last there is a gathering place to preserve
our history,
a permanent campfire
around which our stories will be told.

BEST EVER FAMILY REUNION

9

GOLD AND CORRUPTION IN THE BLACK HILLS

10

Who owns the Black Hills?
Depends on who you ask.
An 1868 treaty says the Sioux and Arapaho people own it.

Why?

Spoils of war won by great Sioux Warrior Chief, Red Cloud.
He defeated the U. S. Army, stopping wagon trains moving
into Indian territory. Negotiations followed. Thirteen tribal
nations spoke their truth. Seven government peace
commissioners listened and signed before thirty witnesses.
Peace lasted until 1874. Then the U. S. seized the land.

Why?

Gold was discovered in the Black Hills of South Dakota and
Wyoming. Thousands of fortune seekers invaded Sioux lands.
The government offered compensation in 1877.
The Sioux refused, quoting Lakota Chief, Crazy Horse,
"One does not sell the earth upon which the people walk."
The lands guaranteed to them by treaties with the
U. S. Government were not for sale.

So, who owns the sacred Black Hills?
The Supreme Court ruled in 1980 that the United States had
acted in bad faith. Compensation was set at $102 million.
The settlement has appreciated to $1.3 billion today,
representing only a fraction of the gold, timber and other
resources removed. The Sioux will not accept any payment.

They do not want money. They want their sacred Black Hills
as promised in the 36-page Treaty of Fort Laramie, signed
May 25, 1868, one-hundred-fifty-one years ago.

The treaty is on exhibit at the Smithsonian National Museum
of the American Indian, along with many others dishonored
and disregarded by the United States government.
"It is my wish that the United States honor this treaty,"
says Chief John Spotted Tail (Sicangu Lakota,
citizen of Rosebud Sioux Tribe), great-great-grandson
of Spotted Tail, one of the treaty's original signers.
Like Crazy Horse, the Chief believes,
"One does not sell the earth upon which the people walk."

GOLD AND CORRUPTION IN THE BLACK HILLS

LET THERE BE LIGHT

(A Sestina)

They live in poverty on barren ground.
Rusted car bodies litter the countryside.
Clotheslines sag in desert heat.
They have no running water or electricity.
Stench of sewage infuses each breath of air.
They are the First People of our land.

The Navajo have lived long in their homeland.
They honor its sacred ground,
beasts of the forests, birds of the air,
even its sunburned countryside,
often bereft of electricity,
broiling in summer heat.

Anger boils too, discussions heated.
Government has failed to provide this land
with the barest necessity – electricity.
Dead generators foul the ground.
Outhouses outnumber trees in Navajo country,
overpowering Desert Rose in summer air.

Then hope arrives, a promise, airtight,
that air-conditioning can replace sweltering heat,
but electric poles may alter the countryside,
change the face of the land.
Warriors win – lines will go underground.
At last, they will have "prayed-for" electricity.

A team of volunteers with its electrical
equipment arrives; digging, hammering fill the air
as precious lines are buried in the ground.
They work in 100-degree heat,
penetrating the concrete-hard land,
preserving, as much as possible, the countryside.

Rusting generators disappear from reservation country.
Warriors welcome the arrival of electricity.
Connection to civilization comes to Navajo land.
The scent of Desert Rose once again fills the air.
Elders are able to escape the scorching heat.
Moccasined feet dance to bless the wires underground.

Sacred ground now illuminates homes across the countryside,
offers indoor plumbing, relief from heat--all thanks to electricity--
filling the air with endless possibilities for the First People of our land.

LET THERE BE LIGHT

(A Sestina)

13

WHO ARE THE IMMIGRANTS?

14

We are called Indians,
Native Americans,
First People,
Indigenous Americans.
We answer to all, if spoken with respect.

But don't name your sports teams after us.
Don't teach your children to play games
of Cowboys and Indians unless
the Indians are sometimes the good guys too.

Oh, and if you are barring immigrants from this land,
remember, unless you answer to one of those names...
Indians, Native Americans, First People,
Indigenous Americans...YOU are an immigrant here.

We let you in and taught you to survive in the wilderness.
You repaid us by stealing our lands,
and murdering sixty-three million of us.
What gives you the right to decide who stays and who goes?

Instead, it's time to pay it forward...
to allow struggling and threatened families in,
to share in the bounty of the land of the free
and the home of the brave,

as we allowed you in,
and shared with you.

CHAPTER TWO
GOING HOME AGAIN

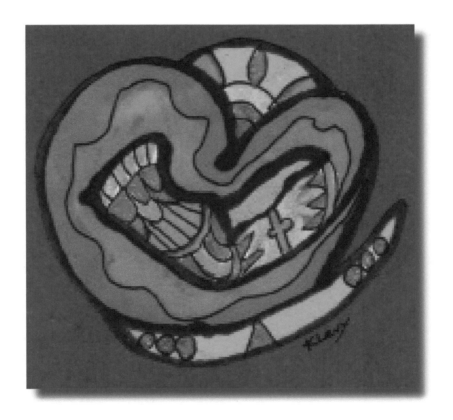

We can go home anytime we choose
by closing our eyes and remembering
those faces from our past, their laughter,
and the love that surrounded us.

ZINNIAS

FOR

REMEMBRANCE

16

I planted zinnias for loved ones today,
in shades of pink and fuchsia and yellow,
in earth warmed by spring sun,
softened by tears and April rains.

I planted zinnias today and marigolds,
in gold and Tuscan orange,
seeds to grow and remind us,
spring's rebirth follows winter's darkness.

I planted zinnias and marigolds today,
for parents, for siblings,
for friends, gone too soon,
for my love, my soul mate.

I planted life today
for all of us they left behind,
who will love, protect and nurture each other,
as we remember,
as we always remember.

Twinkling lights greet me as I crest the last hill,
heading down into the small town I used to call home.
It's Christmas Eve - stores are still welcoming customers.
People scurry along the narrow street,
clutching packages and excited children.
Light snow glitters in the streetlights.

Much has changed in this small town
nestled in the West Virginia hills,
since I left it, fifty years ago.
Many buildings are empty, signs faded,
Mosries Dress Shop, Murphy's Five & Dime.
A Honky Tonk's beacon still promises food and fun.

My Uncle Virgil's barbershop is long gone,
along with the movie theatre
and the Moose Lodge across the street.
The outskirts of town reflect the changes-
a new Kroger Store, a sprawling subdivision,
fast food restaurants, a Dollar Store.

My destination lies five miles east,
a small frame house at the end of a steep drive,
surrounded by fruit trees and evergreens.
The windows are dark, the rooms empty.
My mother and father are long gone,
along with glowing trees and welcoming hugs.

My brother and his family await my arrival--
three doors away--a lifetime away from this silent house.
I sit for a few minutes, savoring the stillness,
allowing the memories to dance through,
awakening the soul of this place,
a place called home.

A PLACE
CALLED
HOME

17

NIGHT SYMPHONY

The music of memory…

…Hound dogs howling in the distance,
begging to be set free for the chase.

…Crackling in the pot-bellied stove
as Dad adds more wood.

…Tick - tock of the clock
that will startle me awake at six for school.

…Mom's absent-minded humming
as she finishes the last of the day's chores.

…Patter of rain on the tin roof,
promising the spring garden will grow.

…My younger brother's peaceful snoring
in the bed across from mine.

…Muddled voices I can't quite identify
drifting from the television in the living
room.

…Seven-thirty train whistle,
warning it's time for dreams.

The music of childhood…
the music of home.

Courage doesn't always roar.
Sometimes it is the quiet voice
at the end of the day, saying,
"I will try again tomorrow."

That quiet voice is my brother's.
Every day, for five weeks, Carl has
awakened, struggled from his mobile chair
into his truck and gone off to radiation.

This is just his newest challenge.
He fought through a kidney transplant,
heart surgeries, a brain aneurism,
diabetes, and now, cancer surgery.

When I called him on Sunday,
he was in his chair on the front porch,
filling pots with seeds and plants
for vegetables and summer color.

I called him to listen,
to sympathize with his pain,
and to remind him there is only one
more horrific week of radiation to go.

I called him to say, "I love you."
I came away with reassurance the
human spirit can endure and endure.
His boundless hope lifts me up.

COURAGE

19

LIVING OFF THE LAND

My dad's garden was his pride and joy.
He fed the earth with fertilizer, seeds, and plants.
In turn, the earth fed his family through the
frozen Appalachian winters.

As soon as the Farmer's Almanac decreed in the spring,
potato planting began, the plow eating through the black earth,
carving out rows of trenches for seed potatoes,
saved from last year's harvest and carefully cut,
making sure each piece had an *eye* from which a
new potato would sprout and grow.
Dad would go down the rows,
covering the pieces gently with his big, calloused hands,
like a blessing of anticipation and appreciation.

Corn planting was next.
A handful of corn kernels, a walk down the plowed rows,
carefully spaced to allow walking room
and an equal amount of sunshine for each corn stalk.
When the corn was ripe in midsummer,
we would strip the ears from their stalks,
remove the husks, cut the corn from the cobs
and stuff the kernels into glass canning jars,
but not before roasting some of the fattest ears,
drenching them in butter and gorging.

When green beans were ripe for picking,
Mom and I would sit in the porch swing, and string bushels
of tender beans, breaking them into canning-sized pieces.
Their bright green jars would join the yellow jars of corn
on sturdy cellar shelves.

Tomatoes were a summer delicacy.
When tomato vines produced more fruit than we could eat,
they too, were canned or juiced.
Between summer garden crops, we picked apples,
scoured the woods for blackberries or raspberries,
and concocted a colorful assortment of sinfully sweet jellies
and jams to top Mom's fat biscuits.

By Thanksgiving the cellar would be filled
with burlap bags of potatoes and crunchy apples,
rainbow-hued jars of vegetables and fruits,
and a freezer full of meat and fish
from Dad's hunting and fishing expeditions.
.
My dad dug coal in the mines when there was work,
but his true love was tilling the soil.
Home was a simple frame house, heated by a pot-bellied stove,
with a bucket well on the back porch, an outhouse on the hill behind.
We didn't have much money,
but Dad, Mom and the land kept us fed and warm.

LIVING OFF THE LAND

21

SHARI AND SANDI

22

F   Forever friends from the age of six
    when we braved the big, yellow school bus
    on our first day of school.

R   Reality check as we left the safe cocoon
    of middle school for junior high -- that dizzying
    world of boys, football games and boys.

I   Imagination reigned--we dreamed of high school dances,
    double-dating with our handsome boyfriends.
    When none materialized, we went to the junior prom together.

E   Ever after - our promise of eternal friendship.
    Graduation came and went, and so did we,
    to college and marriage and babies and life.

N   Never forgotten - the slumber parties, the jukebox dances,
    borrowing each others' clothes, hours on the phone,
    as our parents complained, threatened, and finally, gave up.

D   Distance prevailed. We built lives on opposite sides
    of the country. Visits every few years, Christmas cards,
    condolence cards as we each lost parents, one by one.

S   Sweet coincidence - Sandi's retirement move to Arizona.
    My unexpected visit there. A reunion after twenty years.
    A hug and forever friends simply picked up where they left off.

At six, my world was black and white,
without those shades of gray.
My truth was sometimes mine alone,
no mind what others say.

I knew I would awaken each morning to the delicious aroma of bacon and hot biscuits.
I didn't know my mother rose at five a.m. to start the fire in the iron cooking stove.

I knew if we planted corn in spring, we'd have roasting ears with butter in summer.
I didn't realize the kernels had to be watered and weeded – it was all garden magic.

I knew on July 4th, we'd pig out on watermelon and homemade strawberry ice cream.
I didn't question why Daddy hung the flag and saluted the old men riding in the parade.

I knew on Saturdays, Daddy and my uncles drank from bottles in brown paper bags.
I didn't understand why Mom and the aunts got so mad at them.

I knew my favorite cousin went away and returned months later with a baby.
I didn't figure out why the aunts and uncles whispered about her and that tiny baby.

I knew school was a magical, safe place, filled with books I couldn't wait to read.
I didn't know those imaginary worlds would carry me through so many hard times.

I knew from our Bible School stories, there were poor children in far-away lands.
I didn't realize until I entered junior high school in seventh grade that I was poor too.

I knew my grandparents adored me and treated me like a beautiful princess.
I couldn't know how much I would miss that unconditional love when they were gone.

At six, my world was black and white,
the good, the bad, the strange.
My truth was often mine alone,
to create — rearrange.

CHILDHOOD TRUTHS AND SECRETS

THE "RUN FOR THE WALL"

24

They descend on my small hometown
in the Appalachian Mountains
like swarms of noisy mosquitoes -
five hundred strong,
motorcycles of every size and noise decibel,
bound for the Vietnam Memorial, Washington, D. C.

Piloted by veterans of Vietnam, Iraq, Afghanistan
and every skirmish in between,
they thunder down the mountain,
into streets lined with families,
unemployed miners, disabled in wheelchairs,
all applauding, cheering, waving American flags.

For many years, this small coal mining town
has welcomed the "Wall" vets who travel
to D. C. each year to honor their fallen comrades.
They feed them, house them, and honor their sacrifices.
The hillside behind them is covered with flags,
representing the war casualties from the state.

An event that started with a small welcome picnic,
has become a town-wide celebration of remembrance.
Vets look forward each year to this reunion
with their West Virginia friends.
This year, the mobile Vietnam Casualties Wall
draws silent visitors and tears.

The "Run for the Wall" assures that those Americans
who paid the ultimate price for our freedom
are remembered and revered.

Summer *ripens* into fall in the hills.

The last of the garden harvest is done.
Cellars overflow with bulging burlap bags of
potatoes, apples, nuts; rainbow-hued jars filled
with vegetables and fruits line wooden shelves.

Air grows crisp and pungent with the scent
of burning leaves; southbound geese cry goodbye.
The scarlet crown of autumn signals briefer days,
longer, cooler nights under eider down quilts.

Pale sun scatters frosted light on bare ground,
where lately yellow poppies spread gold filigree
on the hillsides. Green time is gone.
Wild roses and fragrant sage are dead.

Frost nips the dawn.
Forest beasts seek homes;
their heartbeats still.
Human beasts rest,

as autumn *marches* across the summer hills.

**SUMMER
LEAVES THE
HILLS**

25

WHEN OLD FRIENDS MEET

We're grayer, we move a little slower,
but our eyes meet as the young women
we were when we first met and bonded
as we searched for truth, ourselves,
and the path for our lives.

Decades of life have rolled over us
since those thirty-something days.
Marriages have come and gone.
Children were born and grew up.
Careers began, peaked, moved on.

Addresses have changed.
Distance has complicated reunions.
The voice on the other end of the phone line
is less recognizable, but no less welcome.
Christmas letters are eagerly read and re-read.

Life achievements or blunders are of no importance.
Later, we may notice the smile wrinkles,
the extra pounds around our once-24-inch waists.
But at this moment, the eyes have it,
glistening with happy tears, when old friends meet.

You will sit on the swing,
I will sit in the chair,
and the fragrance of lilacs
will hang in the air.

I will tell you a story
I've told you before.
We will laugh (like the last time)
and tell a few more.

Then perhaps we will say it
or perhaps we will not,
but we will be thinking
this very same thought…

that it's good to be known
and it's good to be there,
where the fragrance of lilacs
hangs in the air.

WHEN WE ARE OLD

27

D ivorce is like surgery.
 It excises moments, years,
 and a piece of your heart.

I t changes people forever,
 stealing peace, stealing stability,
 branding us with a Scarlet D.

V ery few escape unscathed.
 Yesterdays creep into tomorrows,
 trapping us in a cycle of remembrance.

O ver it," some proclaim loudly in public,
 crying silently into their pillows in private.
 Denial, denial, denial.

R arely, a partner plots a "do-over,"
 triggered by seeing the "Ex" with a new love.
 Jealousy temporarily clouds sanity.

C lever the "Ex" who can smile nonchalantly,
 stand there, head high, tears swallowed,
 muttering platitudes instead of screaming obscenities.

E ver after, isn't, sometimes.
 Sometimes we don't recover from the Scarlet D.
 Sometimes we get it right the second time around.

They tumble out of my house the same way they tumbled in -
sippy cup and mugs in hand, mini iPads under their arms,
giggles echoing in the quiet, frosty after-Christmas morning.

Adaline, the ten-year-old, big-sisters the little ones into their car seats.
Emma, the bright-eyed, six-year-old middle child,
tenderly tucks her new Cabbage Patch baby into the seat belt.

Zachary, the all-boy, five-year-old force of nature,
waves a new truck, his irresistible dimpled smile
displaying the space where his new front teeth will soon be.

Daughter-in-law, Amy, and son, Steven, circle the van,
tightening seat belts, squeezing in last minute snack bags,
fastening those ever-present iPads to the backs of seats.

They are like a well-oiled machine, packing every space,
carefully tucking newly acquired Christmas presents
into their digitally equipped Santa sleigh on wheels.

Their visit has been a whirlwind of hugs, food and laughter…
getting reacquainted with grandchildren who are suddenly taller,
and squeezing in quiet catch-up talks by the fire after kids are in bed.

As I watch the firelight play on Steven and Amy's much-loved faces,
I silently lament the fact that they live out of daily hugging distance.
Kudos on these parents who could have stayed home by their own fire.

The kids wave as our Christmas visit comes to an end
and the Santa safari van moves on to the next grandparent visit.
Happiness is…all of us together…for three glorious days.

**CHANGING
TRADITIONS
…THE SANTA
SAFARI**

29

A Very Scary Fairy Tale

Once upon a time, there was a beautiful land
suddenly attacked by a silent, invisible enemy.
Thousands of citizens perished.

The People could no longer go to work or school.
They were quarantined at home with their families,
pets, assorted electronic devices and Netflix.
What were they to do?

First, they cooked all the food in their freezers,
including, in some cases, items hoarded since Y2K.
When they ran out of freezer dinners, they foraged in the
pantry to create culinary surprises from lima beans and Jell-O.

They cleaned their overflowing closets and drawers,
unearthing treasures, taxes from 1980 - 2019, and junk.
The trash and recycle workers left them hate mail,
but they kept right on pillaging and purging.

About week six, they emerged to discover SPRING with
bright, clear skies and no scent of exhaust fumes.
Birdsong filled the air, daffodils danced on strong legs,
and the deer in the back yard had stopped coughing.

The people of the land were so delighted, they
volunteered to stay indoors a few more weeks --
in exchange for toilet paper.

CHAPTER THREE
THE WORLD THE WAY IT IS

We live in a world of haves and have nots.
We live in a world of apathy and idealism.
We live in a world on the brink.
We can ignore it or change it – our call.

LABELS

(Through your lens...through my lens)

I am a seeker of truth.

I am a mother and a daughter.

I am a friend and an enemy.

I am a leader and a follower.

I am a writer and a reader.

I am a creator and a consumer of creations.

I am a giver and a taker.

I am unique and I am the same as you.

I am a study in contrasts.

I am a child of the universe.

My personal shopper daughter
leaves two bags of groceries by my
side door, then texts me, "I'm here."

We chat for a minute across the slab
of concrete. She says, "I wish I could
hug you." I reply, "I'm just glad to see
your beautiful face." She waves and leaves.

I spray the paper bags with Lysol, carry
them inside. I clean the cans and boxes,
put them in the pantry on a dedicated shelf.
I won't use them for several days.

I scrub my hands with soap, while singing
"Happy Birthday" twice. I use my small
stash of Clorox wipes to clean the doorknobs.

This is my new coronavirus normal as a
chronologically disadvantaged human.

SIX FEET
APART

33

WARRIOR

34

(Dedicated to Lynn, who inspired me every day)

She heard the diagnosis and refused to bend or bow beneath the weight.
She submitted to the surgery without a whimper or a "poor me."
Somber-faced friends came to visit. She sent us home with lighter hearts.
She soldiered through chemo and radiation, losing her beautiful blonde hair,
but not her determination or her persistence or her reassuring tone.

When she was strong enough, she donned a sexy wig
and returned to her favorite past-time: belly-dancing.
We all breathed a sigh of relief. Lynn was back.

But so was the angry beast. The cancer returned with a vengeance.
Treatment again. Misery again. Worse than the first time.
She persisted, month after month, hoping for remission.

Then the pain returned.
The words she dreaded from the doctors came...
the despicable, unrelenting, savage beast was still there.

She exhausted every option, as warriors do, fighting 'til the end,
leaving us, who loved her, with a model of never-ending hope,
passion for every day of life, and unrelenting courage.

Namaste, dear friend.

Grinding of chain saws fills the hot summer air.
Felled tree trunks jar the stone-hard ground.
Cries of, "Out below," join the symphony.

Neighbors wander from house to house,
reassuring ourselves that everyone is safe,
that we weren't the only ones attacked.

At 10:20 last night, a whooshing "train sound"
heralded a mini-blast, followed by terrifying thumps
on roofs, splintering crashes on porches and decks.

Lights went out, televisions went dark,
computers went down.
We were left in ominous silence.

We wouldn't know 'til daylight that
trees had been twisted out of the ground,
that neighbors' roofs had been crushed.

Ahead lies a long road of clean-up
with costly, painful repairs.
Future whistling winds will trigger new fears.

Today, an army of chain-saw handlers clears
trees and debris from blocked roads, driveways.
Their grinding is the music of miracles, reminding us

we have survived Mother Nature's temper tantrum.

THE MUSIC
OF
MIRACLES

35

THE VALENTINE DANCE

One by one, long, sleek limos deliver precious cargo,
boys in tuxedos, awkwardly clutching corsage boxes,
giggling girls in rainbow hued gowns,
flitting, like butterflies across the school lawn.

Inside the transformed gymnasium,
the excited young teens take their places,
boys on one side, girls on the other,
waiting expectantly under flower canopies.

The high school band executes a drum roll.
The principal and vice-principal step forward,
each holding a red box trimmed in paper doily hearts.
A name is drawn from each box and announced.

The named boy and girl meet in the center of the room.
The boy bows and presents his corsage gift.
The girl curtseys as he places the flowers on her wrist.
They wait nervously as others are matched and join them.

When each has a partner, the band swings into high gear.
Misty-eyed parents peer from the sidelines
as couples gyrate to their favorite tunes,
awkwardness forgotten in the joy of the moment.

Tonight, no one is left standing on the sidelines.
Tonight, there will be no tears.
For one night, their special-needs children
are just teenagers, attending their first dance.

(Inspired by the dances for special-needs teens,
held around the country and sponsored by the Tim Tebow Foundation.)

He sits alone in his 12 x 14 room,
isolated from fellow-residents,
ignored by his family.

Staff brings food three times a day
but he's afraid to eat it because
they are not wearing gloves or masks.

When he tries to advocate for more safety,
staff calls his family members
and brands him a "trouble-maker."

His contact with the outside world
is the television's grim statistics or
an occasional call from a friend.

Nobody tells him if the evil coronavirus
has invaded his assisted-living premises,
claimed friends. Staff says it's a privacy issue.

So he waits, forbidden to walk past other
closed-door rooms to reach the outside,
breathe fresh air, revel in the birth of spring.

He waits and wonders what lies ahead.
He is past his eighty-fifth year -- reconciled
to dying -- but hoping for more time, for more life.

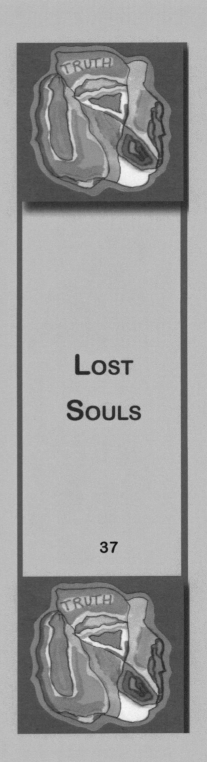

LOST

SOULS

37

TORN THREADS

(a Narrative Poem)

Heroes are not born.
They emerge from the clay of circumstance.

It is 1936.
A 13-year-old boy, living in the quiet
German village of Hammelburg,
is awakened in the middle of the night
and rushed into a waiting car,
along with his parents and younger brother.

A neighbor, fearing for their safety,
risks his own life to drive them to a train.
In a strange city, they huddle behind locked doors
and shuttered windows, waiting for visas.
When they arrive, the Samuels family boards
the S. S. Manhattan, disembarking at Ellis Island, N. Y.

Arnold never sees his grandparents, uncles, aunts again.
They all disappear in the horror of the Holocaust.

It is 1942, one month after the attack on Pearl Harbor.
Arnold, now 19, enlists in the U. S. Army.
He serves undercover on the French/German border,
using his fluent German to recruit informants
whose sleuthing will hasten the end of the war.
He helps to liberate his hometown but finds no family.

The horrors and skeletal prisoners in the ruins of Dachau
motivate him to volunteer for the Counter Intelligence Corps.
His first assignment is to infiltrate an allied POW camp.
Aided by friend and fellow soldier, Henry Kissinger,
he identifies guards allowing Nazi prisoners to escape,
breaks the ring and recaptures many of the prisoners.

Commendations follow as World War II ends.
Voice of America calls and he answers, serving
in the Philippines and Wake Island until retirement.
At 70, he wins a seat on the Ocean Shores, WA City Council.
At 80, he establishes a senior center, which he still runs
at age 95, serving food and friendship to lonely veterans.

From the torn threads of war and dislocation,
Arnold stitched together a remarkable life.

Dedicated to my friend, Arnold Samuels,
who taught me about evil,
and then taught me, by example, about good.

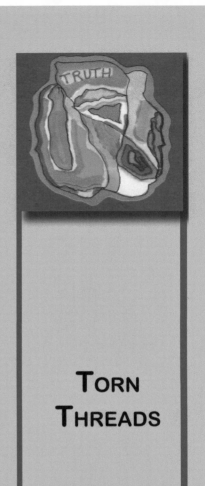

TORN
THREADS

Life In The Shadows

He was a homeless alcoholic
and a drug addict.
He had no one who cared about him.
He lived in the woods behind the shopping center.
He was forty-seven and had been a hard worker
'til construction jobs dried up.

He had a family once, a wife, children.
But his best friends - drugs and alcohol,
drove them away.
When the wages stopped coming in,
the landlord threw him out.
Friends abandoned him, as his family had earlier.

Most days, he stood with a sign by the highway,
begging food to carry back to the tent in the woods.
Sometimes there was enough money to buy dry socks
but only after he bought the cheap wine or drugs
that put him to sleep at night
and awakened him with angry cravings in the morning.

One cold night, the lights of a church drew him in.
The small sanctuary was warm,
the people kind, welcoming.
They gave him food, clean clothes,
arranged for housing and they fed his soul.
He cried when he saw his own shower and a bed.

He began counseling and became a fixture
at every service in the small church.
He did chores for the members to pay back.
One day, he didn't appear at church or his room.
They found him in the woods where he had lived.
His old friends, drugs and alcohol had won.

His church family buried him and grieved his passing.
They vowed to commemorate his life
by doing more to help others like him.
Every day now, homeless in our community benefit
from the program established in his name.
One hopes, he knows he was loved and is not forgotten.

LIFE IN THE SHADOWS

THE SAVIOR ISN'T COMING

42

The room is filled; the mood is grim.

The men are bent, older than their years.
Coal dust lingers in their lungs.
Their women are aged too, from worry,
from struggles to feed families.

These coal miners learned today,
they may lose their health care,
so a tax credit can be given to the wealthy.

The man they believed to be savior,
emerged as Robin Hood,
who steals from the poor and gives to the rich.

He promised a new day for the coal mines.
They believed because they had no other hope.
The emerging truth is devastating.

Their stories unfold as the reporter questions...

...the single mom with a handicapped child,
that child cared for through Medicaid.

...the disabled miner, unable to work,
who feeds his family with his welfare check,
gets his heart medication from Medicaid.

...the widow, physically unable to work but
not quite old enough for Medicare.
What will she do if Medicaid is eliminated?

Fear is a living thing in this room,
a thing that robs people of their dignity,
and sadly, sometimes their lives.

These loyal voters got the memo today.
The savior isn't coming.
The savior doesn't care.
Is anyone out there listening to truth tonight?

Or, are we all in denial - watching "The Bachelor."

CHAPTER FOUR
MIDNIGHT MUSINGS

Dreams or nightmares,
sleeping or wakefulness,
the soul of the night
journeys with us.

Soul Of The Night

"When the deep purple falls over sleepy garden walls
and the stars begin to twinkle in the sky..."
the soul of the night reaches out to envelop us
in dreams of days past and days present...

...dreams of friends who crossed our paths
    and touched our hearts.

...dreams of babes who laughed and played,
    who grew into parents with babes who laugh and play.

...dreams of ambitions thwarted,
    ambitions realized.

...dreams of parents who passed through the veil,
    forcing us to become the reluctant adults.

...dreams of sunlit days and moonlit nights
    in the arms of one true love.

...dreams of laughter, tears, life, death,
    all wander through - carried by the soul of the night.

He came to me in depth of darkness,
Death--majestic in his billowing cape,
taking away people I loved,
destroying my faith in fairness, in futures.

Hope tiptoed in on an autumn afternoon,
whispering…my lost loved ones
were safe and watching over me,
their spirits always in my heart.

Peace rode in on a white horse,
trailing a rainbow on a stormy day,
and carrying a gilded list of gratitudes
that I had ignored or forgotten.

Love enveloped me on a sunny Sunday,
reminding me that she had always been there,
in a friend's hug, in a child's smile,
in a promise kept of a better day.

Happiness skittered in and out,
like a nervous chickadee, wanting sustenance
but fearing to trust the hand that offered it,
'til Time, the Conquerer, brought the ultimate gift,
healing.

TIME, THE CONQUERER

45

AFTERMATH

The days tumble over each other
like scarlet maple leaves in October.
It's morning; it's evening.
Did I eat lunch? I can't remember.

Children come by; friends call.
I don't recall our conversations.
The noise in my head drowns out everything.
The lump in my throat is suffocating.

I sleep but do not rest.
I cry but am not comforted.
I awaken in gray light of dawn,
sheets rumpled, pillow damp.

I reach out but no fingers curl around mine.
I hate the pragmatic voice of truth that murmurs,
"He's gone."

Who is
the face
in the mirror?
Are you mother?
Daughter? Wife?
When did you evolve
from youthful innocence
to dubious wisdom of age?
Who stole precious years,
leaving behind a stream of memories
that fills each night with
technicolor dreams of days long past?
Does the curtain between life and afterlife
become gossamer with time--
tempting us,
beckoning us
to pass through,
join lost loves,
complete
the circle?

THE FACE
IN THE
MIRROR

47

HAPPINESS SITS SOFTLY

48

Happiness is like a butterfly.
The more you chase it, the more it will elude you.
Turn your thoughts to other things.
It comes and sits softly on your shoulder.

At 10, happiness was tangible - a shiny new bike,
'til I saw my friend's bike had a pink basket and mine didn't.

At 20, happiness was a shiny new husband,
'til he became a soldier and went to Korea for a long year.

At 30, happiness was a shiny new dream house,
'til dreams were shattered and the house was left behind.

At 40, happiness was children and family life,
'til infidelity reared its ugly head.

At 50, happiness reappeared, in the form of a new soul mate.
I nurtured it, hoping it wouldn't fly away.

At 60, happiness was a home together.
I thanked the universe every night.

At 70, happiness was replaced by her alter ego, pain.
Death marched into Happy Valley,
leaving behind fear and destruction.
I wondered if life's pieces could be glued back together.

Happiness crept back, after a time, not as shiny, still elusive,
a meadowlark's song at dusk,
a grandchild's laughter,
a peaceful heart.

Like the butterfly on a summer day,
happiness sits softly on my shoulder.

The color red is powerful.
The color blue, soothing.
The color yellow, cheerful.
But purple has a soul.

Purple clothed pharaohs,
emperors, and kings,
during life
and in the afterlife.

In ancient lands,
amethyst stones were sacred,
worn only by those
considered to be gods.

Purple saw birth and death,
famine and plenty,
cruelty and compassion,
through eons of man's struggles.

When you look at purple,
it seems to look back at you
with the wisdom of the ages.
The color purple has a soul.

PURPLE

HAS A

SOUL

49

TIME'S
TIGHTROPE

Where does it go…
the priceless time we're given?

We embark on the journey
with confident enthusiasm.

Where are they written…
the rules for living and loving?

Nobody tells us we create
our own happily-ever-afters.

Where is it proven…
that adulthood is a desirable goal?

We reach the middle
just trying not to fall off.

Where are they hidden…
the secrets of aging gracefully?

We approach the end with hard-won wisdom
that the tightrope walkers behind us
don't want to hear.

Darkness tiptoes in on silent feet,
spreading shadows
in the hollow corners of the room.

I am prepared for this stealthy foe.
Lavender-scented sheets envelop me.
Sound machine transports me to the seashore.

Eyes close behind my velvet sleep mask.
One at a time, tired, tense muscles relax,
starting with toes and inching up to my neck.

I wait to melt into that delicious place,
between wakefulness and deep sleep,
that place of dreams.

Nothing. I feel wide awake.
I try counting backwards from one hundred.
This time, my best sleep remedy doesn't work.

Moving to remedy #2, hot tea and honey,
I wander, barefoot, down the dimly lit stairs
and into the kitchen.

Warm water oozes between my toes.
I flip the light-switch. Nothing happens.
The room is pitch black and eerily quiet.

Then I am in my bedroom,
snuggled in my lavender sheets,
soothed by the sounds of surf, breaking on the shore.

The next day, I awaken early.
Refreshed and hungry, I hurry down to the kitchen.
Water oozes between my toes.

The glare of morning sunlight reveals a flooded kitchen,
a guilty dishwasher,
and a shorted-out light switch.

**THE ART
OF
DREAMING**

51

My Cinderella Night

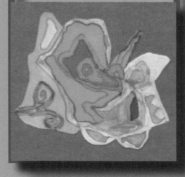

I can hear eight thousand Mary Kay beauty consultants
cheering on the other side of the velvet curtain.
I pause at the bottom of the stairs to the stage,
waiting to hear my name called,
awaiting my turn in the spotlight.

I advance a step, then another,
two more stairs to go,
two more sales directors to walk into the spotlight,
then it's my turn.
I've worked all year for this glorious night of celebration.

I lift the hem of my long, purple sequined gown,
carefully lower my silver high-heeled foot
onto the last rung of the staircase.
I hear a ripping sound and feel the zipper go.
The curtain opens.

I am standing in the spotlight,
my beautiful gown around my ankles
as eight thousand voices gasp,
then burst into sympathetic applause,
which is interrupted by the shrieking of my alarm clock.

Saw a ship today,
sails against the sky.
Wished to go along,
'cross the waters, fly,

to some ancient land
only seen in dreams,
with grand waterfalls,
cool, clear, rushing streams.

You will be there too,
sailing by my side,
shrieking to the wind,
"This is one wild ride."

When the sun sinks low,
shadows fill the sky,
we will wade ashore
as the night birds fly.

Shelter will await,
candlelight and wine.
Plan tomorrow's sail,
smiling as we dine.

TAKE ME
AWAY

53

LOVE IS A PERFECT PINEAPPLE

54

A glance in my rear-view mirror
reveals an unfolding family tableau.
Feeling a little guilty but curious,
I sit transfixed, unobtrusive, watching.

Two people lift an elderly man into a wheelchair.
The woman covers his gaunt frame with a plaid blanket.
A young man adjusts a white mask over his nose and mouth.
I wonder...wife and son?

They trundle him into the grocery store.
I follow, my own list in hand.
We separate at the door,
but cross paths again later as I wait at the check-out.

The wheelchair shopper is carefully surveying pineapples.
He picks up one, turns it, sniffs it and puts it back.
Again, choose, scrutinize, sniff, reject.
For once, I'm glad my check-out line is slow.

After four rejections, he nods his head,
places the chosen fruit into the basket.
I catch a glimpse of twinkling eyes
and know he is smiling behind the white mask.

Over his head, the woman and man exchange smiles.
I feel tears welling in the back of my throat.
Happiness today is the search for a perfect pineapple.
Love is allowing the adventure to happen.

Chapter Five
Mighty Mother Nature

Every part of the earth is sacred.
We are its caretakers.
Generations to come will judge
whether we succeeded or failed.

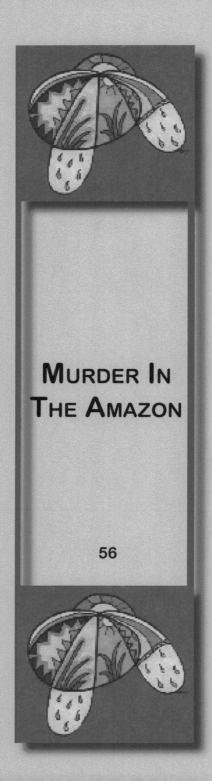

MURDER IN THE AMAZON

One first becomes aware of the silence.
No bird calls or creature rustlings.
Acid scent of burnt peat smothers
the clean, moist air of the rain forest.

The Amazon is burning.
The lungs of the planet beg for relief.
The native protectors of the forest have
been overwhelmed by greedy farmers

who, encouraged by the government,
set fires to clear the land.
Money blinds them to the truth of
the murder they are committing…

murder of plants that may hold the key
to cures for disease and suffering;
murder of wildlife that cannot escape;
murder of native peoples' homeland.

Thousands of acres are imperiled.
Hundreds of miles away, cities are
plunged into darkness by stifling smoke
which can be seen from space.

This destruction of one of the most
diverse habitats on the planet, provider
of 20% of the world's oxygen,
goes largely unchecked and unlamented.

Apathy is killing the rain forest.
All humanity will pay the price.

Mountains cry in spring,
giving up their icy crown,
for humble blossoms.

Tears fill rocky creeks,
home to large bass and catfish,
bound for spring's table.

Sun warms dark hollows.
Lady slippers grace the crown.
Spring triumphs once more.

SPRINGTIME BATTLE

(Haiku)

57

PARADISE FOUND

A rosy dawn emerges from the sea,
trailing silver across the waves.
The ocean is a deep azure blue and warm as bath water.
Palm trees nod in the breeze.
Melodic birdsongs punctuate the silence.

A scarlet hummingbird shares my morning mango,
then flits away.
Hermit crabs drag their shells over the sand,
gathering at water's edge.
Tiny lizards entertain, sailing effortlessly from rock to rock.

Goats, brown, white, and black,
nibble the leaves beneath my porch perch.
Codie, the green-eyed island cat,
waits politely for morsels from the lunch tables,
then wanders off to complete his daily ablutions
in the lazy afternoon sun.

I, too, am lazy, pretending to read,
but snoozing in my chair.
The snorkelers and scuba divers return,
looking like creatures from the Black Lagoon,
comparing notes on sightings of octopus,
barracuda, and giant rays.

As day fades, I follow a narrow,
rocky goat path to the top of our island world,
to "ooh" and "ah" at a fuchsia sunset spectacle in the round,
laced with ribbons of gold.
I long to stay here forever.

I contemplate the return home tomorrow
to a post 9/11 world,
wondering if I will ever feel this safe, this peaceful again.
As the last trace of color fades from the finger-painted sky,
I wander back down the hill.

With moonlight streaming through my open window,
and surf crashing on the shore,
I drift off, grateful for one more perfect day in paradise.

PARADISE FOUND

MOTHER NATURE'S FURY

(Narrative Poem)

Sheets of rain slice the black sky,
sending streams of water down the driveway.
Hail bounces off the sliding glass door,
collecting in small piles on the patio.
Shrieking wind sends chills through my soul.
Tall pines in the back yard
yield and bend to the will of a mighty master.

Hurricane Isabel has arrived, on time,
and more powerful than predicted.
A sharp crack, like a gunshot,
sends me running to the front door
in time to see the ancient maple across the street
succumb with a crash that rattles my windows.
Pooling water is creeping up my front walk.

It's time to leave.
I take one last look around.
I've moved as many things as possible upstairs.
The heavy furniture is propped precariously
on plastic boxes, raising it off the floor.
Dining room chairs are perched on top of the table
Low kitchen cabinet shelves have all been emptied.

Don is waiting impatiently in the motor home,
concerned that flooded roads will prevent us from leaving.
Our cars have been moved to high ground.
There's nothing more I can do.
I wonder what I'll find when I return.
Images of an earlier storm, Hurricane Floyd,
torment me as we abandon the neighborhood.

Hurricane Floyd's three days of pounding rain in 1999,
eroded an earthen dam near my townhouse complex,
emptying a lake and sending its waters
rushing into our streets and homes.
Residents were removed from second story windows
in rowboats manned by emergency personnel.
Cars stranded in the parking lot filled to the top with water.

We were not allowed back in for three days.
My downstairs was water-soaked and mildewed.
Furniture, appliances, everything, had to be dragged
to the curb, along with carpet and drywall.
The upstairs had not flooded but everything was damp and moldy.
Anything salvageable had to be cleaned, moved out and stored.
The final blow was news that my homeowner's insurance would pay nothing.

Home for three months was our 22 ft. motor home,
parked outside my house,
as Don, my son, Steven, and I tried to rebuild.
Anguishing scenes of Floyd replay in my head as we flee Isabel.
The storm rages the next day and news is grim, trees down, power out.
I insist on driving home the third day,
still unable to get definitive reports of damage to Jamestown 1607.

We have difficulty getting into town.
Local roads are still blocked with downed trees.
It looks like a war zone.
At the entrance to 1607, we find standing water and tree damage.
My heart is in my throat as we approach my street.
The water/debris line is at my doorstep but the interior is dry.
I collapse in tears.

MOTHER NATURE'S FURY

(Narrative Poem)

61

Love Is Strange

A chickadee approaches the window cautiously,
flying back and forth, fluttering closer,
teasing, backing off, then CONTACT,
pecking the glass as he helicopters in mid-air.

For three days, again and again,
he zeros in, pecks at the bird in the glass,
retreats a few feet, assesses the situation,
then buzzes in one more time.

I admire his persistence but worry
he will dive-bomb the glass and hurt himself.
I close the blinds, trying unsuccessfully
to dull the reflection that keeps him coming back.

I'm sure the chickadee is male,
based on memories of my own experiences
with a pre-teen boy with a crush.
Subtlety was never his strong suit either.

He also relied on teasing and running away,
persistently chasing me around the playground,
once stealing a peck on the cheek,
then hiding behind a tree to watch me blush.

They're not so different,
the chickadee and my first suitor.
They were saying the same thing.
See me. See me.

They cross the street slowly,
twelve of them,
tiny heads up,
flat feet planted firmly
on the pavement.
Mother goose leads the parade.
Father goose guards the rear.
Cars stop.
Drivers relax.
Everyone smiles.
A tiny moment
in a busy day,
a reminder
of why we're here.

Life renewing life.

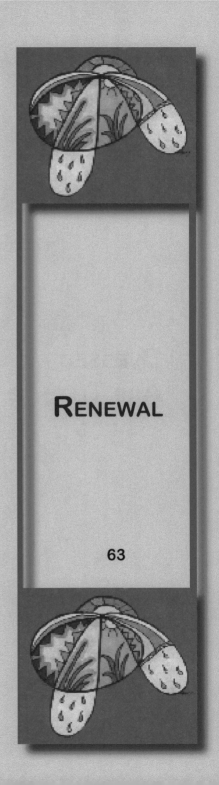

RENEWAL

BLESSED ARE THE BIRDS

Outside my window, all is white...
drifting, blowing powder has turned to ice crystals,
covering every unsuspecting object.
The thermometer gleefully
declares five degrees above zero.
A gray sky gives no promise that the sun will ever reappear.
Perhaps it is really gone forever,
as our early ancestors believed.

Looking out my kitchen window,
I notice a gathering of chickadees,
pecking patiently at ten inches of frozen snow.
No food in sight but apparently
hope springs eternal, even in the hearts of chickadees.
As I sprinkle the snow with seed,
their happy chatter reassures me that life goes on
and the sun will probably come out tomorrow.

I pause in midst of busy, working day,
to watch a turtle cross the gravel street.
I roll down glass to bathe in fragrant heat
of honeysuckle's sweet, warm breath of May.

The turtle moves along at turtle's pace,
head bobbing crazily, without a care.
He looks around and sniffs the springtime air,
then moves ahead, without a hint of haste.

My weighty stresses slowly slip away.
I watch him reach the tall, thick lemon grass,
and breathe a sigh that he is safe at last.

Perhaps we all should slow the race of days,
to sniff the air and feel sun's healing beams,
and lose ourselves in peaceful turtle dreams.

TURTLE DREAMS

(Italian Sonnet)

65

GOATS IN TREES

I've traveled here and traveled there, seen a lot of sights,
mountains, rivers, dazzling sunsets, even city lights.

Saw Tulum, and Cancun, spent a week in Granada.
Toured Alaska, the Yukon, a trip to Jamaica.
We sailed on a tall ship, hiked the Narrows at Zion.
Then we climbed Chichen Itza; the ruins are Mayan.

We flew off to Hawaii, explored every island.
I wanted to stay there, learn to surf and get suntanned.
While traveling through the islands, we witnessed a strange sight.
Goats nibbling on tall grass on a flat roof in sunlight.

Happy goats on a rooftop! Didn't know that could be.
Even stranger, in Morocco, their goats can climb trees.
Saw pictures, can't believe it. Argan fruit must taste great.
Farmers then extract oil from the seeds where they ate.

Goats in trees -- Disney magic? No, they did climb up there.
Tourists flock to Essouira to look up and stare.

I watch them creep across the slippery ledge,
staying close, one behind the other, soldiers on patrol.
The rescuer in front stops to check on a fallen comrade,
leans over him for a long moment, then moves on.

Three more times he pauses, leans over,
then moves past the still bodies, his guard following,
each of them careful not to get too close
to the edge of the precipice.

The fifth time they pause, there is movement.
Quickly, the guard comes forward.
The rescuers place themselves on either side
of the wounded and carry him to the edge of the ledge.

A chain of helpers passes him down, one by one,
'til he is safely on the ground.
As I watch them carry him into the tall grass,
I find myself wishing humans were as compassionate as ants.

RESCUE

67

THE AWESOME ANIMAL ALPHABET

68

A   is for Ardvark.
B   is for Bear.
C   is for black Cats,
    who doze in my chair.

D   is for Doggies.
E   is for Eel.
F   is for big Fish,
    who eat little krill.

G   is for Gators.
H   is for Hare.
I   is for Insects,
    who go where they dare.

J   is for Jackal.
K   is for Kid.
L   is for Llamas,
    who spit. Yes, they did!

M   is for Mongoose.
N   is for Newt.
O   is for Otter,
    whose coat is a beaut.

P   is for Parrot.
Q   is for Quail.
R   is for Rhinos,
    who never get mail.

S   is for Seahorse.
T   is for Terns.
U   is for Upas,
    who hide in the ferns.

V   is for Vixen
W   for Whale.
X   is for Xantus,
    whose wings never fail.

Y   is for Yabby
Z   is for Zho.
    Have no more letters.
    AND THAT'S ALL I KNOW!

(Upa…a rainforest bird; Xantu…a
rare hummingbird;
Yabby…European green woodpecker;
Zho…offspring of yak and cow)

There once was a cricket named Don,
who liked to hide out in the john.
One day he forgot
to lock down his spot.
One flush and now Donny's long gone.

Oops!

(Limerick)

69

A Tale Of Nancy And Not Cat

(Narrative Poem)

He emerged from the woods on a chilly day in early spring
when golden forsythia was bursting from winter branches,
a thin, tuxedo black cat with white nose and paws.
Nancy watched him survey the yard, sniff the air
and cautiously approach the deserted bird feeder.

He considered the seed on the ground, turned up his nose,
wandered closer to the back porch, then turned and ran
back to the woods. This ritual continued the next day
and the next. On the fourth day, Nancy met him
at the birdfeeder with chicken scraps and a bowl of milk.

He gobbled it down and retreated to the woods.
Day five, he was back, waiting at the feeder.
Reluctantly, Nancy fed him again, telling him,
"This is the last time. You are NOT my cat.
Go away and find your family."

A neighbor, coming to visit, witnessed this exchange,
laughed and said, "I think he IS your cat."
The next day, she returned with a gift bag of cat food.
Thus, began a strange game between Nancy and Not Cat.
She put out food, he ate, and both went to their separate corners.

One day, she heard a loud hissing and saw Not Cat chasing
away a family of raccoons intent on tearing down the birdfeeder.
His reward was extra milk. Hers was a brief rub across her legs.
The next day, he sat beside her on the porch steps.
She reached out to stroke his head. His claws left a bloody stripe.

She jumped up, pointing a bleeding finger, "YOU are NOT my cat!"
Not Cat ran into the woods and was gone for days.
Nancy wondered if he had gone home, wherever that was.
Life went on. Then one day, he was back at the feeder, skinnier.
Nancy saw him, hesitated, decided to ignore him.

When she didn't bring food, he marched up the steps to the door,
silently pressing his nose against the glass, peering inside.
Nancy left the room, thinking he would go back to the woods.
He didn't. It was a stand-off. At dusk, he was still sitting by the door.
Defeated, Nancy brought out chicken, cat food and milk.

The next day, she heard loud meowing from the area of the birdfeeder.
Assuming Not Cat was still hungry, she carried out a plate of food.
When she bent down to put the dish on the ground, something caught her eye,
shimmering in the sunlight. It was her favorite earring, gone missing days ago.
Not Cat purred and rubbed against her legs as if to say, "See! I AM your cat."

From that day forward, he was.

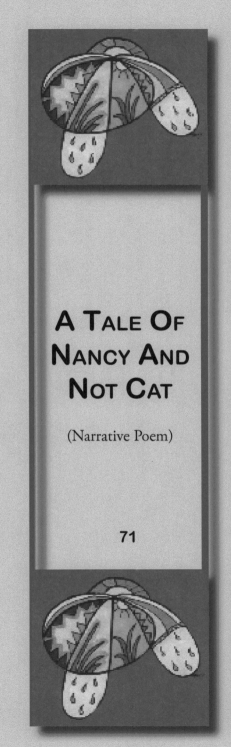

A Tale Of Nancy And Not Cat

(Narrative Poem)

71

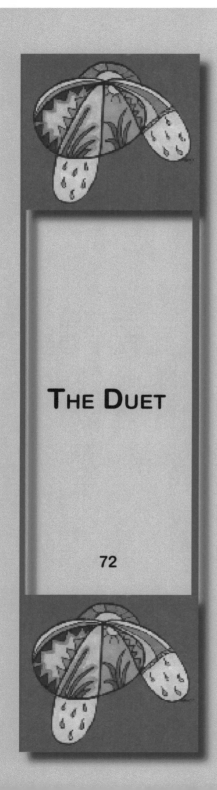

THE DUET

72

He sang and sang, sang and sang.
Occasionally he sputtered.
Then I heard a second voice
chime in to join the other.

Duets soared throughout the night,
passionately crescendoing.
Sweet love song or rival fight?
I hoped for happy endings.

Suddenly, concert ended.
Silence filled the summer air.
Love lost, won, quarrel mended?
Only those two crickets care.

The South Pacific boasts a tree
with bark in rainbow hues –
a Eucalyptus, rare, indeed,
seen only by a few.

Fairies in blue or lavender
can hide among the trees.
Yellow clad nymphs frolic and play,
amidst the birds and bees.

Only a child's eye sees beyond
the multi-colored limbs
to spot the giggling fairies
at dusk when sunlight dims.

"Join us," they tease and tempt the child.
"We only want to play."
Children who climb the rainbow limbs,
disappear, parents say.

But on a full-moon night, you'll hear
patter of dancing feet,
giggles of fairies and children
echoing down the street.

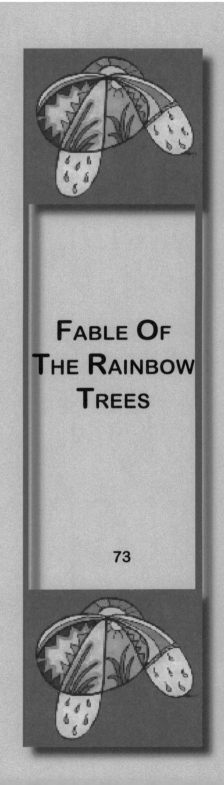

FABLE OF THE RAINBOW TREES

SUMMER'S LAST HURRAH

74

Cotton candy clouds drift across the azure sky.
Playful waves kiss the beach, then retreat,
leaving behind shell treasures.

Tiny sandpipers skitter along the water's edge,
helping themselves to unsuspecting sand fleas.

A light October breeze reminds me,
summer is winding down, a fleeting luxury.

The sun's warmth on my shoulders is medicinal,
temporarily curing all aches and pains.

A flock of geese, headed south, honks goodbyes
that echo in the silence of afternoon.

I soak in the sun, the solitude, the peace,
grateful for summer's last hurrah.

CHAPTER SIX
GIGGLES AND GRIPES

Laughter can bring together...
parents and children,
friends or adversaries.
It is the drug that heals.

A Song To Spring

(To the tune of London Bridge)

Yellow pollen fills the air,
fills the air, fills the air.

Clogs our nose and gums our hair.
Falalalalala.

Then the rain comes falling down,
falling down, falling down.

Softens up the winter ground.
Falalalalala.

Makes the green grass grow and grow,
grow and grow, grow and grow.

Forces us to mow and mow.
Falalalalala.

Now I need to end this song,
end this song, end this song.
Glad you all could sing along.
Falalalalala.

(Phase one…The Honeymoon)

Bob is sophisticated, exciting,
and new to my life.
We are in the getting-acquainted stage.
I'm learning his background and history.
He's learning my habits and expectations.
So far, neither of us has been disappointed.

I get up early, stay up late, need little sleep.
Bob's available around the clock,
always there when I want to pour out my heart.
He's dependable so far, but I'm slow to trust.
I've been burned before.
I'm waiting to see if he's fully committed.

Time will tell if we are a match.
or if we are just human and P. C.,
ever-evolving ships, passing in the night.

(Phase Two…Honeymoon's Over)

I have a computer named Bob,
who sometimes sits down on the job.
I warned him today.
He will have to pay.
Tomorrow I call the Geek Squad.

MY LOVE AFFAIR WITH BOB

77

RENT-A-

FRIEND

78

In Japan, there is a way
to find a friend to share your day.

Rent-a-Friend will search for you,
to find a friend that's fair and true.

Grandma types to hear you vent?
There's absolutely one for rent.

How about a wedding date,
or just someone who likes to skate.

Want a friend who likes to cook,
while you sit back and read a book?

If you're gay and can't tell Mom,
a rental girlfriend goes along.

Platonic is the key word here--
no hanky-panky, that is clear.

Charge your card and then press send…
next day, you'll have a brand-new friend.

(Dedicated to all those technology-challenged Grandpas)

I watch you deftly manipulating your iPad,
and marvel at the differences between
our twelve-year-old lives, sixty years apart.

I would have been outside, playing cowboys and Indians.
You are battling digital aliens to save the planet.

I spent my summers barefoot, going swimming in the creek.
You are planning to attend computer camp at the junior college.

I wished in vain for a Red Ryder BB Gun for Christmas.
You expected and received your first iPhone.

At twelve, you're already worrying about getting into college.
At twelve, I was free to play and dream and wander.

I don't know which way of life is better, yours or mine,
but if I had to choose, I'd go for the dreaming and wandering.

Otherwise, I'll have no wild stories to tell when you come to visit.
Everybody knows – telling tall tales is in the Grandpa job description.

GENERATION
GAP

79

ODE TO BEING

CHRONOLOGICALLY

DISADVANTAGED

(My Love/Hate
Relationship
with Aging)

80

My eyes now see double.
My knees creak and crack.
My back aches in rain storms
I can't eat Big Macs.

I cannot climb mountains.
My kayak is gone.
I won't wear a swimsuit.
I don't mow the lawn.

A few things, however,
are freeing and fun.
There's more time to travel,
just chasing the sun.

I write in my pjs,
curled up by the fire,
while housework gets finished,
by someone I hire.

I ignore without guilt,
those meetings and clubs.
They now run without me,
while I get back rubs.

On bright, sunny mornings,
I wake up at nine
and thank the Great Spirit,
I still have my mind!

"I hate aging!" a friend whined today.
"Me too! Me too!" I hastened to say.

I hate...
sensible shoes...pounds I can't lose;

doctor appointments...hemorrhoid ointments;

being called, "ma-am"...not saying damn;

bags 'neath my eyes...political lies;

my swim suit bod...which once was mod;

forgetting friend's names...long trivia games;

a back that aches...a car that breaks;

cleaning the house...seeing a mouse;

calling Cox cable...their response--fable;

getting bad news...missing life clues.

I hate...
losing my friends...that all things end.

I shared with my friend this old southern line...
"Hey, honey-chile, like some cheese with that whine?"

**PARDON
ME WHILE I
WHINE**

81

Becky has vertigo, now needs a cane.
Can't find a cause and the cures are inane.

Kay broke her hip and is now in rehab.
Pat goes to Mayo in March for new labs.

Janie is late for important meetings,
plus, can't recall if she's the one leading.

Judy just fell and has broken her arm.
She keeps insisting, "I'm fine. There's no harm."

Peggy's back problems were caused by a dog,
who dragged her along on his morning jog.

Debi's about to replace both her knees.
Marilyn's breathing is tinged with a wheeze.

Ann has decided she can't drive at night.
We'll eat early dinner, while it's still light.

Our lunch conversation centers around
competent doctors someone has just found.

Now when the phone rings, I grab keys and purse,
wait to see which of my friends needs a nurse.

We've been through divorces, babies and wakes,
there for each other, whatever it takes.

Shoes multiply – like rabbits.
You start out with some sturdy Birkenstocks,
maybe a pair of Capezio heels; the next thing you
know, your closet is overflowing with pink ballet
slippers plus six pairs of multi-colored tennis shoes.

My mother had the worst case of shoe proliferation
I've ever seen. I blame it on the West Virginia climate.
All that snuggling in the winter resulted in multiples
of pastel spring sandals and flirty jelly flip-flops.
We evicted two hundred pairs from closets and under beds.

Sadly, the inbreeding results in symptoms of instability.
Shoes wander off, but never in pairs, so you're forced
to go to work in one brown loafer and one chocolate flat.
After my last move, I unpacked shoes I'd never seen before.
I have an unproven but logical theory— space aliens.

I applied for a grant to study this footwear phenomenon,
thinking it could be my lasting contribution to society.
So far my only response was a happy face emoji.
I assumed multiplying shoes would trigger lots of publicity,
but Russia and an orange president stole my air time.

SHOE

SHOCK

83

A Woman's Place

...In The 1950s

...In 2020

84

In 1955, an anonymous article, called the Good Wife's Guide, was published in several women's magazines. I became aware of it when I was cleaning out my mother's house after her passing and found it in a stack of old papers. The fact that she kept it says a lot about the female mindset of that time and what they believed was expected of them. The Guide inspired this free verse poem. The first line of each stanza is from 1955. The second is my 2020 rebuttal.

Have a delicious meal ready when your husband comes home from work.
Show me a man who can cook and I'll run away with him tomorrow.

Dress, do your hair and take fifteen minutes to rest before he arrives home. You must look your best.
I happen to like my sweats, and the dog ate my hair brush.

Try to be interesting for him. It's your wifely duty.
Steven bit the new neighbor kid and Shannon threw up in your shoes.

The house should be immaculate when he arrives, and a drink waiting.
Are you home already? I've been binge-watching "The Crown" all day.

Teach your children to be obedient and silent when their father is home.
Kids! You promised me you would not slime your father!

Listen to him, for his topics of conversation are more important than yours.
Sue from Book Club says your friend, Joe, is sleeping with the babysitter.

Don't complain if he comes home late or stays out all night because he is the master of the house and you have no right to question.
No, you can't come in and yes, I did have the locks changed.
Your clothes are at Goodwill and your motorcycle's in the pool.

Listen, listen, Dr. Suess!
Did you know the goose is loose?

Saw him on Mulberry Street.
Tried to catch him by both feet.

Then he tried to Hop on Pop.
I yelled, "No! No! Stop! Stop! Stop!

Red Fish, Blue Fish chimed on in,
"We could teach him how to swim."

Cat in Hat knew what to do.
We tuned in to hear the clue.

"Green Eggs and Ham," he told us.
"He'll give up without a fuss."

Goose ran faster, talking low,
"No! Oh, The Places I'll go."

HAPPY BIRTHDAY DR. SUESS!

If We Could Turn Back Time... 100 Years

A lot of us would already be dead.
Life expectancy was forty-seven years.

We would be moving at a much slower pace.
Speed limit was ten miles per hour.
We could buy gas and drugs at the same time.
Fuel for cars was only sold in drug stores.

We would be communicating via letter.
Only 8% of people had a telephone.
Your doctor probably had no college education.
He learned through on-the-job training.

We washed our hair only once a month,
with borax or egg yokes.
The average worker earned $200 a year,
BUT, 18% of households had at least one servant.

Pharmacists touted heroin
as a "perfect guardian of good health."
Marijuana, heroin, and morphine were available
over the counter at the corner drugstore.

Canada passed a law prohibiting poor people
from entering their country.
Our president is vowing to adopt that regulation.
Can we send him back one hundred years?

She lay very still in her glass casket, eyes closed, waiting.
The clip-clop of horses' hooves drew nearer, then stopped.
Dry leaves crunched under Prince Charming's feet.
A fragrant breeze stirred Sleeping Beauty's blonde curls.

The prince carefully lifted the flower-covered lid.
Beauty held her breath, willing her body to be still.
Charming was overcome by her delicate beauty.
He bent down and gently touched her lips with his.

Nothing happened. Beauty did not awaken.
Once more, he kissed her. Nothing.
Presuming her to be dead, an anguished Charming
rode away into the depths of the thick forest.

When all sounds had faded into the distance,
Beauty climbed from her golden casket and
ran in the opposite direction, stopping only long enough
to trade the frilly gown for a pair of pants and linen shirt.

Tucking her long hair under a cap, she could easily
pass for a young boy, out for a walk in the countryside.
She retrieved her notebook from its hiding place and
sat down to finish her story…

"Once upon a time, there was a young woman who
didn't want to marry Prince Charming or become a princess.
Instead, she wanted to write books, about magic spells,
wicked witches and damsels who didn't need rescuing."

THE SECRET LIFE OF SLEEPING BEAUTY

87

I Am

Woman

A puzzle to solve.
Charming and cunning.
Resilient and courageous.
Bringing changes to the world.
Making life's wild ride more fun.

INDEX

HighTide
Publications, Inc.

ABOUT THE ARTISTS

KAYE LEVY and VIVIEN MANN are multi-media artists, both known for their unique styles.

KAYE lives on the water in a picturesque village near Gloucester, Virginia. This is her first collaboration with the author.

You can reach Kaye at kardsandstuff@gmail.com

VIVIEN resides in the red rock country of Arizona in the little town of Cottonwood.

She and Sharon have worked together on four other books, *Herman the Hermit Crab and the Mystery of the Big, Black, Shiny Thing; Revolt of the Teacups; Tapestry;* and *Daughter of the Mountains.*

You can see her art and jewelry at www.designsbyvivien.com.

About the Author

SHARON CANFIELD DORSEY has published fiction, non-fiction, juvenile fiction and poetry in magazines, newspapers, journals and anthologies. She is a member of National League of American Pen Women, Inc., James City Poets, Poetry Society of Virginia, and the Chesapeake Bay Writers. Sharon has received awards from Christopher Newport University Writer's Conference, Poetry Society of Virginia, National League of American Pen Women, Gulf Coast Writer's Association, and Chesapeake Bay Writers. She was a winner of the Art Lit Project, which displayed her poetry on the sidewalks of the city of Williamsburg, VA.

Sharon is a Senior Sales Director of 40 years with Mary Kay Cosmetics, Mom to son, Steven and daughter, Shannon, and grandmother to Adaline, Emma and Zachary.

Other Books by Sharon Canfield Dorsey

Children's Books

Herman, the Hermit Crab and the Mystery of the Big, Black, Shiny Thing;
Revolt of the Teacups;
Buddy and Ballerina Save the Library;
Buddy the Bookworm Rescues the Doomed Books

Memoir

Daughter of the Mountains
Road Trip (a travel memoir)

Poetry

Tapestry
Captured Moments (an anthology)

VISIT SHARON'S WEBSITE AT WWW.SHARONCANFIELDDORSEY.COM

YOU CAN CONTACT HER BY EMAIL AT SHARGYPSY@AOL.COM